Tommy's Veterans Day Flag

This book belongs to:

Tommy loved the big, bright flag that flew at his school.

Every morning he watched it waves in the wind. He dreamed of one day carrying the flag himself.

One sunny morning Tommy's teacher, Mrs. Turner, told the class about Veterans Day. She said it was a day to honor the men and women who served the country.

Tommy raised his hand. "What does it mean to serve the country?" he asked.

Mrs. Turner smiled and said: "It means they protect our freedom, like your grandpa did."

That afternoon, Tommy visited his grandpa.

"Grandpa, what does Veterans Day mean?" Tommy asked as they sat on the porch.

Grandpa smiled and said: "It's a day to remember the people who were brave, like my friends and me when we helped keep our country safe."

"Were you scared, Grandpa?" Tommy asked.

"Sometimes," Grandpa said, "but being brave means doing the right thing, even when you're scared."

That night Tommy lay in bed thinking about what his grandpa said. He wanted to be brave, just like him.

The next day at school Mrs. Turner made an announcement: "This year, one student will carry the flag during our Veterans Day assembly."

Tommy's heart skipped a beat. He dreamed of being the flag bearer, but he wondered if he was brave enough.

After school Tommy asked Mrs. Turner: "How do you choose the flag bearer?".

She replied: "I'm looking for someone who shows respect and understands what bravery means."

Tommy thought about his grandpa and what he had learned. He whispered to himself: "I want to be brave like Grandpa."

At home Tommy helped his grandpa in the garden. Grandpa told him more stories about his time as a soldier and Tommy listened carefully.

One evening Grandpa showed Tommy how to fold the flag neatly. "It's a way of showing respect." Grandpa explained.

The day of the Veterans Day assembly finally arrived. The gym was filled with excited students and proud teachers.

Tommy saw the veterans sitting in the front row, including his grandpa. His heart raced as he thought about the flag.

Mrs. Turner stood on stage and began speaking. "Today we honor those who served our country with bravery and courage." she said.

Tommy's hands felt sweaty as he waited to hear who would carry the flag. Mrs. Turner continued: "We have chosen a special student for this important role."

Tommy held his breath.

Mrs. Turner smiled and said: "Tommy, would you come forward and carry the flag for us today?"

Tommy couldn't believe it! He walked slowly to the stage, feeling a mix of excitement and nervousness.

With careful hands Tommy took the flagpole.

The gym became quiet as everyone watched him carry the flag high.

As he walked, Tommy thought about his grandpa and all the veterans who had been brave for the country.

He looked at his grandpa in the audience and saw him smiling proudly.

Tommy's heart filled with joy. He was honoring his grandpa and all the veterans who had served.

After the assembly Grandpa gave Tommy a big hug. "You made me proud today, Tommy." he said softly.

Tommy smiled. "I wanted to be brave just like you, Grandpa."

Grandpa chuckled. "You were more than brave today. You showed respect too."

Tommy realized that being brave wasn't just about doing big things. It was about honoring those who had done them before.

Every Veterans Day after that, Tommy thought about his grandpa's stories. He remembered the bravery and kindness in his heart.

Tommy knew that one day he would tell his own children about what his grandpa had taught him.

And every time he saw the flag wave in the wind, Tommy remembered what it meant to be brave - just like his grandpa.

How can you show being brave at home or at school?

Time to play :)

Veterans Day Word Search

Find these words in the puzzle:

FLAG   HONOR
VETERAN   RESPECT
TOMMY   HEROES
BRAVE   TEACHER
GRANDPA   ASSEMBLY

T	F	L	A	G	H	E	R	O	E	S
O	V	E	T	E	R	A	N	V	T	A
M	G	R	A	N	D	P	A	V	E	C
M	H	O	N	O	R	A	E	T	E	S
Y	E	X	F	R	E	S	P	E	C	T
A	S	S	E	M	B	L	Y	E	P	T
T	E	A	C	H	E	R	E	C	N	D
S	B	R	A	V	E	I	G	N	E	P

Veterans Day Riddles

Riddle #1
I wave in the sky - red, white and blue.
I stand for freedom and honor too.
What am I?

Riddle #2
I am someone who serves the land, with bravery and a helping hand.
I might wear a uniform, proud and strong.
Who am I?

Veterans Day Riddles

Riddle #3
I help people learn about special days, like Veterans Day, in fun, caring ways.
I stand at the front of the class with a smile, teaching kids all the while.
Who am I?

Riddle #4
I'm the one Tommy loves so dear,
A wise hero who's always near.
Who am I?

Veterans Day Rhyme

Tommy's Big Day

Tommy raised the flag up high,
Waving proudly in the sky.
With Grandpa there, he stood so tall,
Honoring heroes, one and all!

Bravery, respect and fun,
Tommy's journey had begun.
On Veterans Day he led the way,
A hero in his own small way!

Veterans Day Matching

Match each word with the correct meaning:

Words:	Meanings:
1. Flag	A. A person who served in the military
2. Veteran	B. Doing the right thing, even when scared
3. Bravery	C. A special day to honor those who served
4. Respect	D. A symbol of our country
5. Veterans Day	E. Showing kindness and care for others

Draw a flag and color it:

Color the medal and cut it out:

Answers

```
T  F  L  A  G  H  E  R  O  E  S
O  V  E  T  E  R  A  N  V  T  A
M  G  R  A  N  D  P  A  V  E  C
M  H  O  N  O  R  A  E  T  E  S
Y  E  X  F  R  E  S  P  E  C  T
A  S  S  E  M  B  L  Y  E  P  T
T  E  A  C  H  E  R  E  C  N  D
S  B  R  A  V  E  I  G  N  E  P
```

Riddles:
#1 The American Flag
#2 A Veteran
#3 A Teacher
#4 Tommy's Grandpa

Matching:
1 = D, 2 = A, 3 = B, 4 = E, 5 = C